PENGUIN BOOKS

Unrecounted

W. G. Sebald was born in Germany in 1944 and died in 2001.
He is the author of *The Emigrants*, *The Rings of Saturn*, *Vertigo*, *Austerlitz*,
After Nature, *On the Natural History of Destruction* and *Campo Santo*.

Jan Peter Tripp was born in 1945 and lives and works in Alsace.

Michael Hamburger is a poet and translator. His *Collected Poems 1941–1994*
appeared in 1995 and his latest volume, *Wild and Wounded*, in 2004.

Unrecounted

33 Texts and 33 Etchings

W. G. Sebald and Jan Peter Tripp

Translated by Michael Hamburger

PENGUIN BOOKS

PENGUIN BOOKS

Published by the Penguin Group
Penguin Books Ltd, 80 Strand, London WC2R 0RL, England
Penguin Group (USA) Inc., 375 Hudson Street, New York, New York 10014, USA
Penguin Group (Canada), 10 Alcorn Avenue, Toronto, Ontario, Canada M4V 3B2
(a division of Pearson Penguin Canada Inc.)
Penguin Ireland, 25 St Stephen's Green, Dublin 2, Ireland (a division of Penguin Books Ltd)
Penguin Group (Australia), 250 Camberwell Road, Camberwell, Victoria 3124, Australia
(a division of Pearson Australia Group Pty Ltd)
Penguin Books India Pvt Ltd, 11 Community Centre, Panchsheel Park, New Delhi – 110 017, India
Penguin Group (NZ), cnr Airborne and Rosedale Roads, Albany, Auckland 1310, New Zealand
(a division of Pearson New Zealand Ltd)
Penguin Books (South Africa) (Pty) Ltd, 24 Sturdee Avenue, Rosebank 2196, South Africa

Penguin Books Ltd, Registered Offices: 80 Strand, London WC2R 0RL, England

www.penguin.com

www.greenpenguin.co.uk

Penguin Books is committed to a sustainable future
for our business, our readers and our planet.
The book in your hands is made from paper
certified by the Forest Stewardship Council.

MIX
Paper | Supporting
responsible forestry
FSC
www.fsc.org
FSC® C018179

Unzerhält first published in Germany 2003
Unrecounted first published by Hamish Hamilton 2004
Published in Penguin Books 2005

3

Copyright © Jan Peter Tripp and the estate of W. G. Sebald, 2004
Translation copyright © Michael Hamburger, 2004

Unzerhält copyright © Carl Hanser Verlag München Wien, 2003

'Wie Tag und Nacht' by W. G. Sebald, from *Logis in einem Landhaus*,
copyright © Carl Hanser Verlag München Wien, 1998

'Tripps Wunderkammer' by Hans Magnus Enzensberger, from
Die Geschichte der Wolken, copyright © Suhrkamp Verlag
Frankfurt am Main, 2003

The Arnolfini Portrait by Jan Van Eyck copyright © The National Gallery, London

Designed by Richard Marston
Printed in Great Britain by Clays Ltd, St Ives plc

Contents

Translator's Note

English-speaking readers of this book could be puzzled or disappointed to find that a number of these texts overlap with those included in Sebald's earlier collaboration with another artist, Tess Jaray, in the book *For Years Now*, published shortly before the author's death. Because this and other complications worried me when Jan Peter Tripp — Max Sebald's oldest friend, ever since their schooldays — asked me to translate these texts, I found it necessary to discover what I could about the genesis of all the texts written after the completion of *Austerlitz*, at a time of crisis in Max's life and work, full of enigmas, conflicts and contradictions he chose not to clarify, just when he was most readily available for interviews that probed matters he would not divulge to his closest friends.

What that crisis was is something I prefer to leave to Sebald's biographers; but the mere duplication of some of these texts for the two projects is out of character in the Max I knew, scrupulous as he was in all his dealings and so meticulous over the editing of his writings that he spent hundreds of hours on the checking of their English versions — and even the finished copy of the English *Austerlitz* he inscribed and gave to my wife, Anne Beresford, contains emendations in his hand, after the book's publication.

Although Max Sebald had given me copies of all his books published since our first acquaintance, he never so much as mentioned the writing of these miniatures to me and gave me no copy of *For Years Now*. It was he who had asked me to translate *After Nature*, when I had translated only one extract from it in connection with a reading at the Aldeburgh Festival. Though we worked together on the editing of the English version and were to meet again at the moment of his death for a joint checking of the final proof, during the last year of his life he would drop only the vaguest of hints about his work, his state of mind and physical health, even his plans and movements. His total reticence about these texts for artist friends and other short works of that period entered into my hesitations over what he called his 'micropoems' in a letter to Tess Jaray but must always have regarded less as an alternative to the prose book he could not write at the time than as components of his collaboration with two very different artists.

The overlapping texts in the two books are also different in wording. Again, I had to establish for myself that the English versions in *For Years Now* were done by Sebald himself, with a freedom or latitude I could not allow myself as a translator of the German texts. No translator's name appears in the book *For Years Now*; and Max had assured his friend Tripp that he would never write a literary text in English, so that Tripp attributed these versions to an anonymous translator other than Max. Another of the conundrums and contradictions I was up against was that in one case, the text attributed to Robert Schumann (p.23), not only the wording but the sense diverged in the English and German texts: the English text has 'only under / a dark sky' whereas the German text sent to Tripp — most probably a later version — has the opposite, 'only / in brightest daylight'.

Confronted with this contradiction, at first I thought that I must trace the source of this quotation from Schumann but could not find it in the small selection I happen to possess from Schumann's copious writings on music, his journals and letters. After reflection the contradiction struck me as one more instance of the freedom from literalness that distinguished Sebald the imaginative writer from Sebald the scholar. This freedom had become apparent to me much earlier, when he sent me his script of his account of a meeting with my wife and me on which he drew — as well as on my book of memoirs — for his *The Rings of Saturn*. Factual accuracy would have called for the correction of a few biographical details in that account, had it not become clear to me by that time that the very nature of all Sebald's writings other than critical essays demanded such departures from the source material — that, in the context, it did not matter at all whether or not his account of my childhood experiences accorded with my recollection of them. The very writing of my book of memoirs had brought home to me that memory is a darkroom for the development of fictions. Whatever Schumann wrote in a document I could not find, Sebald's versions of it will have been drawn from memory and imagination, indivisible as they are; and what is significant in the contradiction is Sebald's reinterpretation of Schumann's words for the purposes of his collaboration with two artists so different — just as my approval of his account of me meant that I was happy to be a character in his work of fiction.

On that first visit to our house Max had also taken photographs — the visual counterparts of the transcription of documents or quotations, and a necessary complement, for Sebald, to his imaginative freedom. That he was an acute observer of things and places is attested throughout his works — even where the photographs inserted do not tally with the texts more literally than these texts do with the artwork they elicited. One little practical instance of Max's sharp camera eyes I am reminded of by seeing peaches now, on a chronically leaf-curled tree I had given up as a casualty, is that on a later visit to our house and garden Max spotted a single peach on this tree I thought would never bear again. This was an invitation to look again at the thing given up; and it points to the importance of seeing in Sebald's works, less for the sake of noting or counting phenomena than as an act of relating ourselves to things otherwise trivial or meaningless.

To return to these texts or micropoems, I must mention that Sebald wrote more of them than either artist could respond to in terms of her or his practice, and left both of them free to select or reject them on these grounds alone. Thanks to the artists, I have photocopies of his handwritten script of one English micropoem given to Tess Jaray and not included in her book, and of eleven such German texts sent to Jan Peter Tripp and not included in his book. As literary texts in their own right, these are not inferior to those either artist could respond to with visual work; but the present book is confined to the collaboration with Jan Peter Tripp.

To the contents of the German book *Unerzählt* I have added my version of a poem by Hans Magnus Enzensberger about an artist not as well known or appreciated in Britain or the USA as in the German-speaking countries and in France, where he lives and works. Not only did Enzensberger contribute a commemorative poem for Sebald to the German editions — a limited edition of thirty-three copies with Tripp's original lithographs preceded the trade edition — but it was Enzensberger who chose to publish those earlier books of Sebald's, beginning with *After Nature* in 1988, which initiated what was to become Sebald's international readership and reputation. It seemed to me that his tribute to Tripp's art might be as helpful to English-language readers of this book as Andrea Köhler's perceptive review article on the collaboration, which connects these late texts — as difficult to classify as all his works — to his earlier publications.

Another addition to the English edition is Sebald's own essay on Jan Peter Tripp, from his book *Logis in einem Landhaus* (1998), not yet published in English. No clue to the collaboration could be more authentic. Beyond that, it shows how even the scholarly or critical writings of Sebald drew on the same sources and centre as his imaginative works. Erudition, to Sebald, was never an end in itself or only a second string; it was food for his widely ranging curiosity, just as personal culture is the deposit of what has passed through our heads and hearts, not necessarily what we can recall without notes and trot out. Sebald's academic discipline or specialization was German literature, with extensions into comparative literature among many other fields of study. Here, though, he wrote as an art historian and critic, with extensions into general aesthetics; and all these extensions serve to take him back to his most personal and immediate concerns. By defending a friend's work and practice against superficial classification, and by minute attention to that work from long acquaintance and sympathy, he tells us more about his own practices in a different medium than he could make explicit in his imaginative works – down to the miniature texts in the present book, written later than the essay and more essentially enigmatic than the larger books of fiction or semi-fiction.

As for the translation of this essay, it was the title that proved more problematic than the text. 'As day and night', the literal rendering of the German title, points to one of the antinomies on which the essay hinges, though the operative word 'different' could be left implicit because 'different as day and night' is an idiom in German. Its English counterpart, 'different as chalk and cheese', is as different as chalk and cheese from the German idiom. So the metaphysical-cum-psychological implications of the antinomy had to be complemented with the characteristically down-to-earth English idiom. But I have just found 'different as day and night' in a work by an American writer, Carson McCullers. So to American readers the German idiom may have become as familiar as the English one. Contrary to the judgements of several British, American and Australian critics of Sebald's writings, I'm pretty sure that he would at least have smiled at the juxtaposition of German high seriousness and English empiricism in the somewhat grotesque duplication I had to perpetrate in my version, introducing yet another antinomy – an inescapable one of usage – into his intricate nexus of distinctions.

What sets these reductive epiphanies apart from the earlier works is not so much their extreme brevity, spareness and seeming casualness, making them like jumbled snapshots of the most diverse occasions and impressions, flashes of remembered moments, but their break with the narrative thread in all the preceding works, not excepting the 'elemental poem' *After Nature*, a triptych of narratives held together only by a subliminal unity of vision and theme. Sebald and Tripp must have had this characteristic in mind when they chose the unusual word '*unerzählt*' for the German title of the book. I had to render this with a word as unusual in English, 'unrecounted', because the more familiar word 'untold' is not only ambiguous but has the primary sense of countless or measureless. 'Untold' would have carried misleading connotations due to the curious etymological proximity of counting and telling not only in English and German but in other languages also. Ambiguities were to be avoided in these particular texts. Where they are suggestive of more than they state, it is not by ambiguity or punning, though both are respectable resorts in poetry more lyrical or more dramatic than these bare bones of remembrance — which, modestly or ironically, Sebald also likened to postage stamps in another letter to Tess Jaray. Postage stamps lose their validity if they have been forged.

In a letter to me, Tess Jaray mentions that Max carried a book of Japanese haiku when he brought her the first of these texts — one possible clue to the model that Sebald may have had in mind for them, only to play variations on the model in his own fashion. The number thirty-three chosen by Tripp and Sebald for their collaboration was finalized in June 2001, when Sebald sent his friend the last of the '33 things reeled off again, enlarged, exchanged, rejected in part, emended etc.', as he put it in a letter to Tripp. That the limited edition of the texts and etchings comprised thirty-three copies is another instance both of the close agreement between the collaborators and of the almost occult, transcendental or even chiliastic proclivities both of them have combined with the most loving attention to the whatness of seemingly trivial things.

About this collaboration, based on long familiarity and exchanges of which Sebald's essay on Tripp's work is the outstanding record, it is enough here to say that Tripp's etchings are of subjects quite as diverse as those of Sebald's texts. The eyes of all these subjects could never have met in a single place or time. All of them belong to a complex of relations shared by the artist and writer. The presence among them of the dog Maurice or Moritz is neither a joke nor an accident. The very name Moritz recalls the close companionship of Max and Moritz in the most famous of all German children's classics, the verse tale with that title by Wilhelm Busch; and the dog Maurice/Moritz, so close to Max Sebald, died not long after Max's early and sudden death.

But I must not ramble into anecdote, reminiscence or interpretation here. Essentially this book is a collaboration between two friends of longer standing than my acquaintance with Max – or with his work, available to me only when I was well on the way to withdrawing from my activities as a critic. My part was to produce plain versions of these plain and cryptic texts, adding only such minimal information as I thought might help English-speakers to see and read this book.

Michael Hamburger

A Parting from Max Sebald

He who was close to us
from far off seemed to have come
into our uncanny homeland.
Only a searching for traces
with a divining rod of words
that quivered in his hand.
Across conflagration sites
and burying places
he followed it,
though to *raving madness*
on Suffolk heaths.
Is this the promis'd land?

Earlier the dark had encroached,
but he moved on,
through all those nightmares
undaunted made his way.
That dust became light for him
we know from three lines alone:
So soundless I glided
scarcely stirring a wing
high up above the earth ...

Hans Magnus Enzensberger

Tripp's Cabinet of Prodigies

Do you see the paintbrush,
the glove, the veined stone?
No, not the pincers over there on the table,
not the brush in the painter's hand
but this glove here,
this very seam, these pincers, here,
this shadow! You got it wrong.
It is not a glove, it is art.
Not that art over there,
but this one here.

You rub your eyes and ask
what are they there for,
this stone with all its veins,
these pincers here, this brush,
not that one over there on the table.

What for? So that at last
you will see
what you did not see.

Hans Magnus Enzensberger

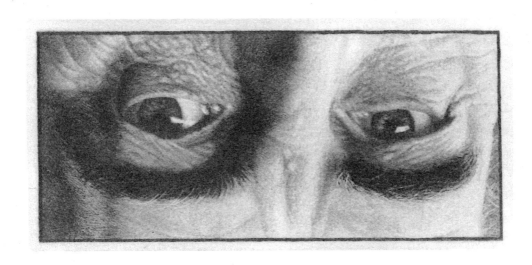

Pliny says

that elephants are
intelligent & righteous
revere the stars
& worship the sun
& the moon

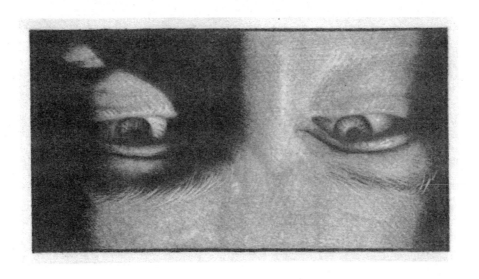

The red

spots
on the
planet
Jupiter
are three-
hundred-
year-old
hurricanes

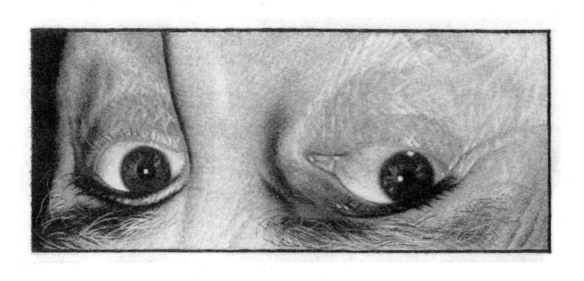

When lightning

flashes drove down
one could see the deeply
folded mountains
& torrential rain
splashed down on the valley

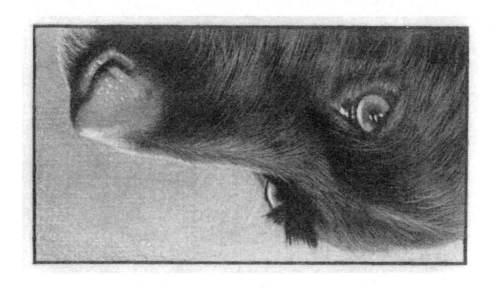

Please send me

the brown overcoat
from the Rhine valley
in which at one time
I used to ramble by night

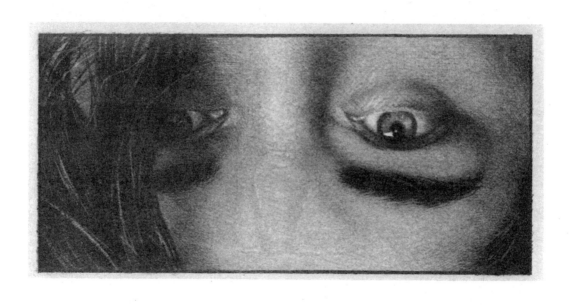

Do you remember

how curiously grey
was the light
when in March we
were on the river island
called Peacock Isle

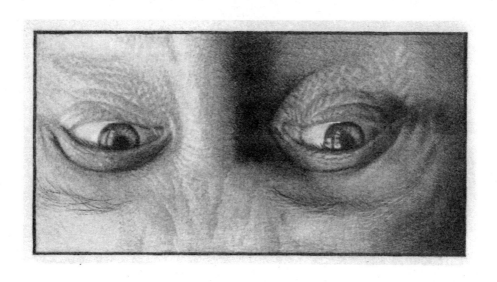

Feelings

my friend
wrote Schumann
are stars that
guide us only
in brightest daylight

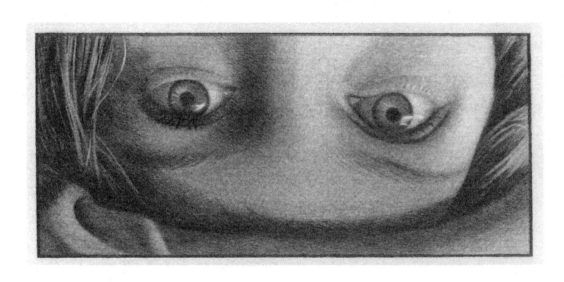

In the darkness

above the mouth
of the Somme the Pleiades
shining
as nowhere else

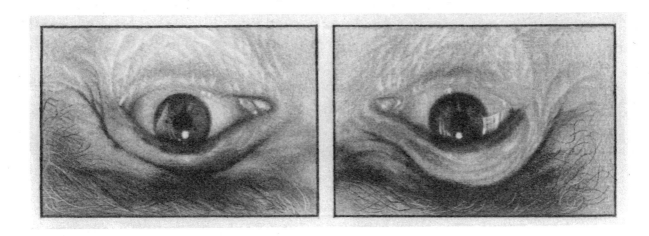

On 8 May 1927

the pilots
Nungesser & Coli
took off from Le Bourget
& after that
were never
seen again

This flight

out of the alcove
these matt lead
panes
sudden flash
of a lance
hardly audible
the scream of terror

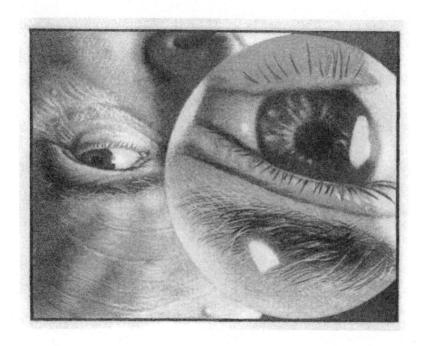

The fruit basket

which the woman carries
in the velvet crook of her arm
the lovely fruit
leafage the apples
& above them all
black black
black

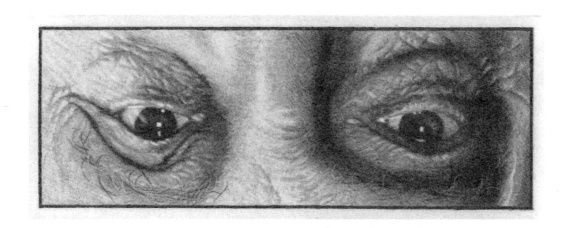

At eleven o'clock

the swastika men
assembled on
the Theresia Meadow
& under the command
of an officer
began to exercise

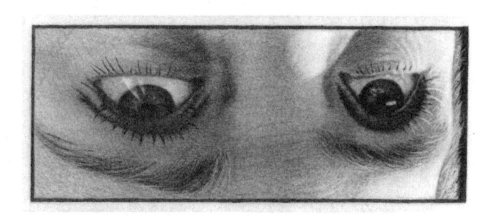

In deepest sleep

a Polish mechanic
came & for a
thousand silver dollars made me
a new perfectly
functioning head

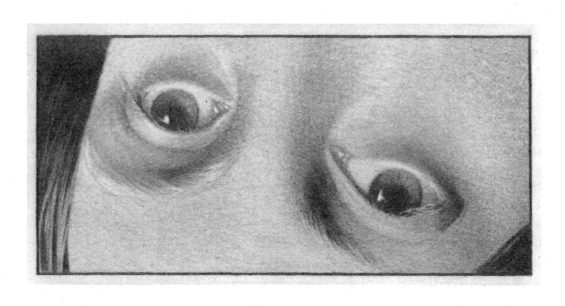

Awakening

her eyelids still
half-closed
she says she has dreamed
of a carpet
all in shreds, in tatters

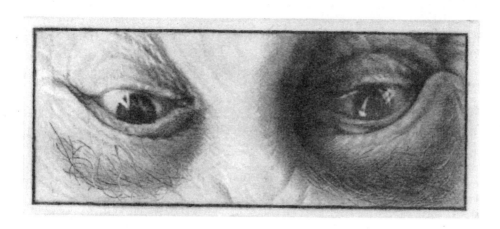

It is

as though I lay
under a low
sky and breathed
through a needle's eye

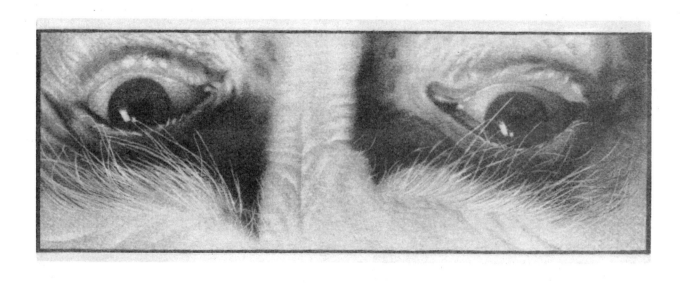

Terrible

is the thought
of our worn-
out clothes

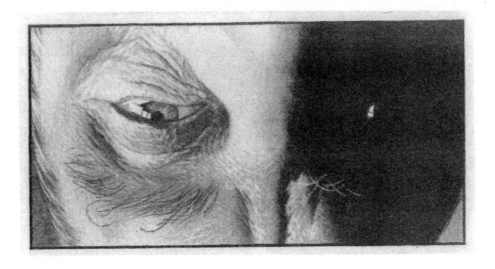

The dor

mouse's shadow
is
death

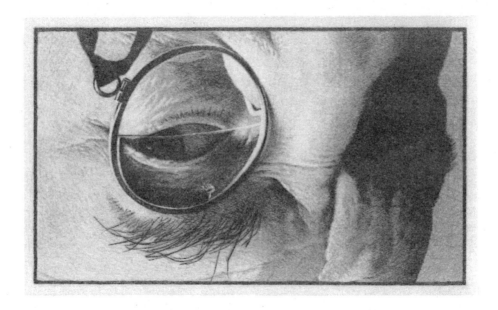

In the Vienna

Josephinum Collection
a sightless
Ethiopian eye
overclouded
by a gauze of
grey silk

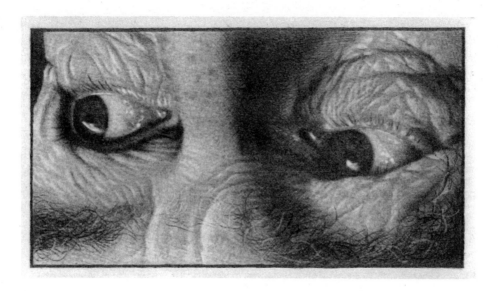

Venetian

reproduction in wax
of the fibre system
in the musculature
of the forecourts
of the heart

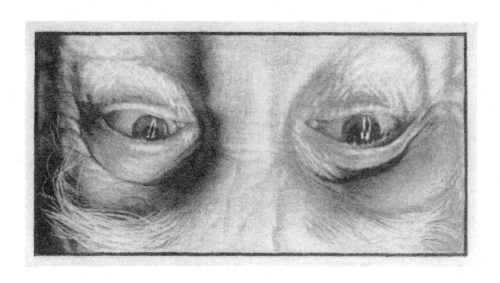

My eye

begins to be obscured
Joshua Reynolds remarked
on the eve of the storming
of the Bastille

Like a dog

Cézanne says
that's how a painter
must see, the eye
fixed & almost
averted

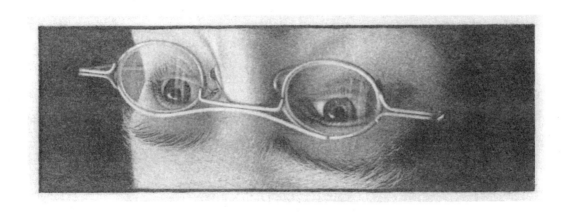

From the foreship

of the brain those
images shot on the wing
as it were into
the cellula memorialis reach
the cooling chamber
memory

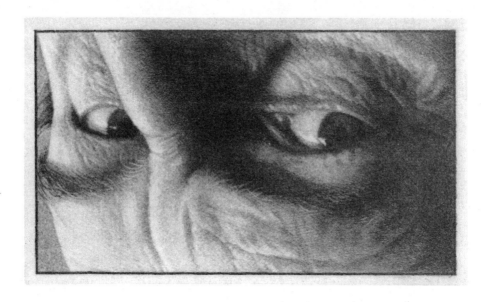

They say

that Napoleon
was colour-blind
& blood for him
as green as
grass

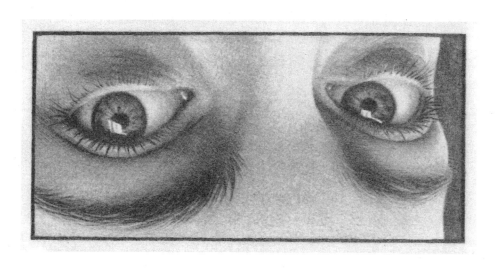

Blue

grass
seen
through a thin
layer
of frozen
water

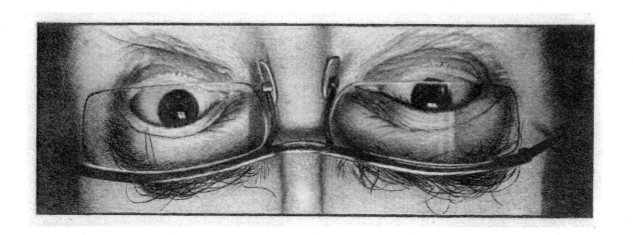

It was a year

so cold
that the farmers
had to cut the corn
wearing fur coats

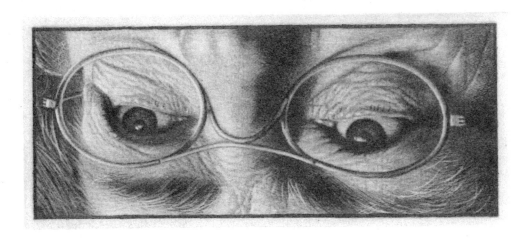

In the dining-car

of the Arlberg Express
sits a man
with a mourning lapel
& calmly, carefully
consumes his
Milanese cutlet

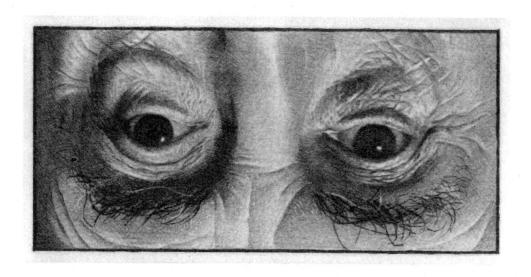

What I see

is human beings for
I see creatures
like trees
save that
they walk about

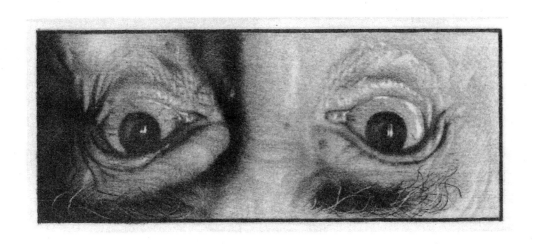

The house

in the night
through the windows
the flickering light of
flames

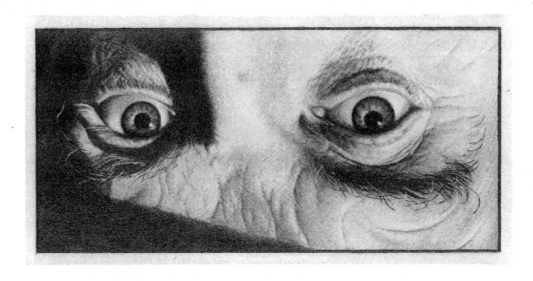

Seven years

in a foreign place
and the cock has ceased
to crow

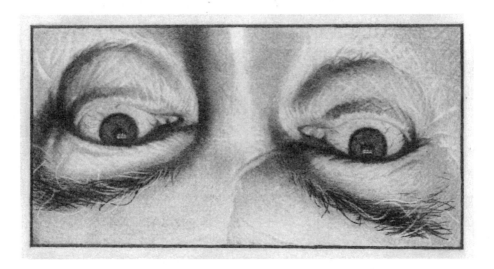

This writing paper

smells
like wood shavings
inside the coffin

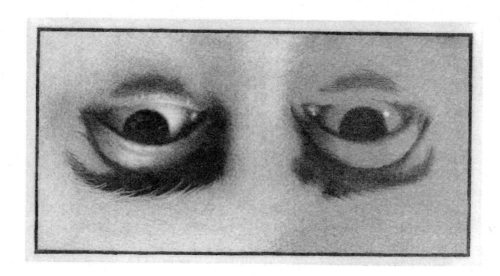

But the time

in which darkness
prevails
that time one
does not see

He will cover

you with
his plumage
&
under his
wing then
you will rest

Unrecounted

always it will remain
the story of the averted
faces

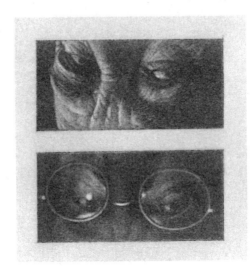

At the end

only so many will
remain as
can sit round
a drum

As Day and Night, Chalk and Cheese: On the Pictures of Jan Peter Tripp

The catalogue of Jan Peter Tripp's work now covers at least a quarter of a century. It includes works on the most various of scales, executed in pencil, charcoal and drypoint, in watercolour, as gouache or grisaille, in acrylic and in oil, all pushed to the limits of the possible or – so it seems to the viewer – beyond them. The pictures of the first three or four years still show the clear influence of surrealism, of the Vienna fantastic realists and of photorealism, bound up with the polemical stratagems of the year 1968; but very soon, during several months spent in the Weissenau psychiatric regional hospital near Ravensburg (in 1973), this polemical trend disappears, replaced by a much more deeply searching objectivity, which by pure representation seeks to sound the phenomena of life, laying bare their formation and evolution. In the process the art of portraiture becomes a pathographic enterprise that admits no dividing lines between what are usually called the characteristic features and the deformations wrought in the subject by pressure of work and inner stress. If the pictures of the Weissenau inmates are to be understood as studies of the resounding emptiness inside the heads of those subjects, no less so are the later portraits and self-portraits in their almost worldless isolationism. Even the representational likenesses of accredited possessors of economic or political power, produced in recent years, have something embarrassed and dislocated about them and correspond implicitly (without any denunciatory intention) with the definition worked out at Weissenau of the human individual as an abnormal creature forcibly removed from all con-

nection with nature and society. The reverse side of this depiction of a species becoming more and more monstrous in the course of a civilization's progress is the abandoned landscapes and especially the still lifes in which – far beyond the events – now only the motionless objects bear witness to the former presence of a peculiarly rationalistic species. What matters in Tripp's still lifes is not that the painter applies his skill and mastery to a more or less fortuitous assemblage of objects but the autonomous existence of things to which, like blindly furious working animals, we stand in a subordinate and dependent relationship. Because (in principle) things outlast us, they know more about us than we know about them: they carry the experiences they have had with us inside them and are – in fact – the book of our history

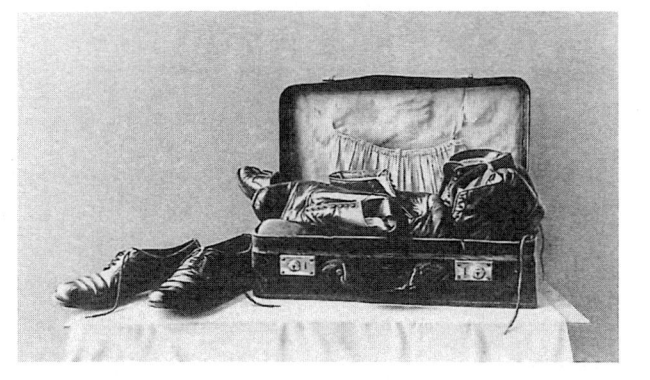

opened before us. In the father's so-called Russian valise lie his son's shoes; the dozen slates and a few faded scrawls evoke a totally vanished school class — images of the past, of what is most enigmatic about a human life. The *nature morte*, for Tripp, much more conspicuously than ever before, is the paradigm of the estate we leave behind. In it we encounter what

Maurice Merleau-Ponty, in his *L'Oeil et l'esprit*, called the *regard pré-humain*, for in such paintings the roles of the observer and the observed objects are reversed. Looking, the painter relinquishes our too facile knowingness; unrelatedly, things look across to us. '*Action et passion si peu discernables*,' Merleau-Ponty writes, '*qu'on ne sait plus qui voit et qui est vu, qui peint et qui est peint.*' ('Action and passion so little separable that one no longer knows who is looking and who is being looked at, who is painting and who is being painted.')

Reflecting on the work of Jan Peter Tripp, in which faithfulness to reality is taken to an almost unimaginable extreme, one cannot avoid the tiresome question of realism. For one thing because everyone looking at a picture of Tripp's is immediately struck by the seemingly unfailing accuracy of the representation, for another because, paradoxically, it is just the stupendous skill that prevents us from seeing his true achievement. The perfected surface offers so little in the way of a clue that even professional art criticism can find very little to add to the layman's expressions of wonderment. There it is significant that such responses are often offered with a shaking of the head, as it were, since unquestioning admiration – just of those schooled in the traditions of the modern and, as far as skill is concerned, generally ignorant practitioners of criticism – is probably accompanied by a disturbing sense of having been taken in by some illusionist working with tricks not to be seen through. In fact Tripp manages not only to interpolate the third dimension into his surfaces, so that, looking, one sometimes thinks one can cross the pictorial threshold, but the material represented, the Cyprus-black cloth of the young Marcel's jacket, his taffeta cravat, the forty-one pebbles and the white snow on the field are so truly present, in the picture,

that instinctively one puts out one's hand to touch it. Ernst Gombrich, in his large-scale studies in art and illusion, reminds us of the story handed on by Pliny of the two Greek painters Parrhasios and Zeuxis. Zeuxis, they said, had painted grapes with such deceptive verisimilitude that birds tried to peck at them. Thereupon Parrhasios invited Zeuxis into his workshop to show him his own work. When Zeuxis made to raise the curtain from the picture panel that Parrhasios had led him to, he noticed that this curtain was not real, only painted. Gombrich then explains how in *trompe-l'oeil* painting the picture's power of suggestion and the attitude of expectation aroused in the viewer reciprocally reinforce each other, and he concludes the section with the remark that the most convincing *trompe-l'oeil* he had ever come across

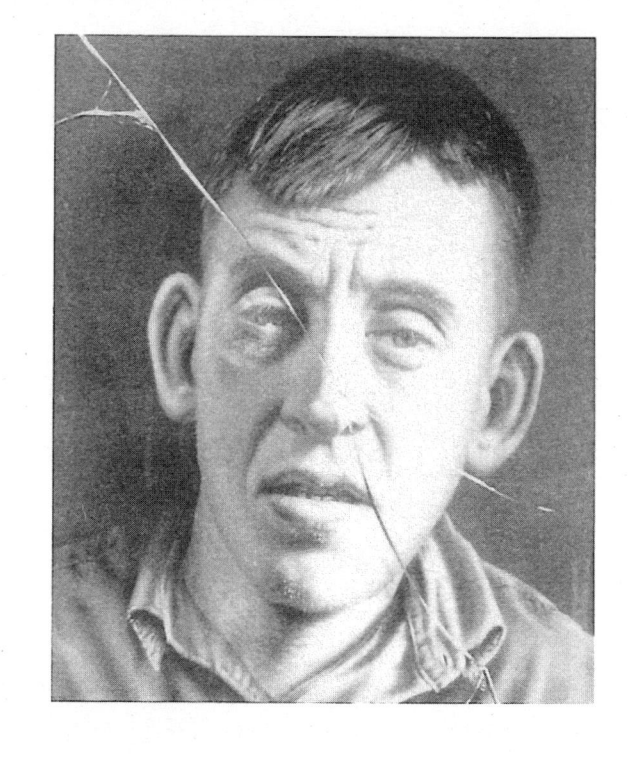

had simulated a cracked pane of glass in front of the painted surface. Well, in Tripp we find both the grapes of Zeuxis and the cracked glass. And yet one would be wrong to see him primarily as a virtuoso of *trompe-l'oeil* painting. Tripp only uses *trompe-l'oeil* as one technique among many, and always – as the watercolour *A Quiet Leap* shows – with the most precise reference imaginable to a thematic implication.

Trompe-l'oeil painting is a manner capable of conjuring forth out of virtually nothing, with comparatively humble means, whether by certain shifts of perspective or by a cunning distribution of light and shades, what is called the '*effet du réel*'. Its most expert practitioners were those known as the *quadratisti*, who roamed Austria and Bavaria in the baroque period to lend to various interiors not especially impressive a palatial aspect, by painting whole flights of columns on to walls and grandiose cupolas on to ceilings. The suspicion of a confidence trick, and a meaningless one, attached to an artistic practice whose effects are randomly applicable – the more so since the rise of photography and the beginnings of modernism connected with that – later extended to the entirety of representational painting. For that reason the assumption that extremely exposed positions can be reached today both in representational art and in the non-representational can hardly be entertained by an art critic, quite especially because photorealism and hyperrealism, with their techniques amounting to objectification, very soon exhausted their resources.

That Tripp's work, almost compulsively, is connected with this already historical trend is a false association. What is worth considering in it is only the implied assumption according to which the inherent quality of a picture by Tripp, just in view of what looks like its purely objective and affirmative nature, probably cannot be attributed to that identity with reality which all its viewers admire without fail – or its photographic reproduction – but in the less apparent points of divergence and difference. The photographic image turns reality into a tautology. When Cartier-Bresson travels to China, Susan Sontag writes, he demonstrates that there are people in China and that these people are Chinese. What may be right for photography, though, is not fitting for art. It needs ambiguity, polyvalence, the resonance of a darkening and illumination, in short, the transcendence of that which in an incontrovertible sentence is the case. Roland Barthes saw in the by now omnipresent man with a camera an agent of death, and in photography something like the residue of a life perpetually perishing. What distinguishes art from such undertaker's business is that life's closeness to death is its theme, not its addiction. It confronts the extinction of the visible world in an interminable series of reproductions by the deconstruction of phenomenal forms. Accordingly, Jan Peter Tripp's pictures, too, always have an analytical, not synthesizing, tendency. The photographic material that is their starting point is carefully modified. The mechanical sharpness/vagueness relationship is suspended, additions are made, and reductions. Something is shifted to another place, emphasized, foreshortened or minimally dislocated. Shades of colour are changed, and at times those happy errors occur from which unexpectedly the system of a representation opposed to reality can result. Without such adjustments, divergences and differences there would be no line of feeling or thought in the most accomplished of depictions. What is more, in studying Tripp's pictures one should bear in mind Gombrich's lapidary assertion that even the realist working with the most meticulous precision can accommodate only a certain number of signs on a given surface. 'And although he may do his best,' Gombrich writes, 'to co-ordinate his colour schemes beyond the bounds of the visible, in the end, when it comes to the representation of the infinitely small, he will have to rely on suggestion. When we stand in front of a picture by Jan van Eyck ... we are convinced that he succeeded in depicting the inexhaustible wealth of detail in the visible world. One has the impression that he painted every stitch in the gold damask, every hair on the angel's head, every fibre in the wood separately, for its own sake. And yet this is out of the question, however devotedly he may have worked with his magnifying glass.' This means that the production of a perfected illusion depends not only on a staggering artistic skill but ultimately on the intuitive steering of a breathless state in which the painter himself no longer knows whether his eye still sees and his hand still moves.

The repeated experience of failing breath in the midst of the utmost concentration on work, of a stillness ever increasing, the paralysis of limbs and blinding of eyes has brought death into the pictures of Jan Peter Tripp. Unmistakable in his early studies

of bones and shells, later, more often, it is concealed
in the ominous objects, in the faces of those portrayed,
in the cracked glass, in the hermetic shape of peb-
bles or in the portrait of a more than fifty-year-old
Kafka. To search him out the painter had to cross a
frontier. On his way to the other side there was also
the dormouse lying one day in front of his house
door. Although it is said that one must paint the dead
quickly, Tripp, in the thick of the chloroform vapour
of putrefaction, spent seven days on that picture in
which the silent message of the unexpected guest is
perpetuated. On the seventh day there was a little
spasm in that lifeless corpse, and a drop of blood the
size of a pinhead issued from the nostril. This was the
true end. Embedded in nothingness, with no support
or background, this animal now hovers through the

air with its bat's ears erect. The black patch of fur
around the eyes has the effect of a mourning crape
or of the dark sleeping-glasses of an air passenger on
a summer night's crossing of the North Pole. We are
such stuff as dreams are made on, and our little life is
rounded with a sleep.

The longer I look at the pictures of Jan Peter Tripp,
the better I understand that behind the illusions of

the surface a dread-inspiring depth is concealed. It is the metaphysical lining of reality, so to speak. In a series of flower paintings, only recently begun, which despite their high degree of realism leave botanical illustration far behind them, this lining comes to the fore. The flowers that at first were to be painted in all the glory of their local colours have turned into muted grisailles in which colour has left only a ghostly trace. They are as though disembodied, in a porcelain rigor mortis. All of them bear female names and so belong to another sex. What is conveyed in the extravagant, diva-like shapes is the almost already forgotten reflection of organic nature. Likewise, in the picture with the green grapes, these are a last sign of life. A peculiarly ceremonial, emblematic style determines the arrangement. The dark background,

the white linen cloth with its embroidered monogram – at once one begins to sense that it has been spread not on a wedding table but on a coffin-rest or catafalque. And painting, what is it, anyway, if not a kind of dissection procedure in the face of black death and white eternity? Variously it recurs, this extreme contrast, for instance, in the chessboard floor pattern of the Belgian billiards picture from Tongeren, which not by chance makes one think that the painter, within the framework chosen for any one work, let himself in for a precarious game in which one false move can easily ruin everything. Already in one of his earliest pictures the 'cobalt-blue madder-lake ball' rolls towards a night-side vanishing point, and in all the later pictures the most complicated chess gambits and evasions are enacted, to and fro between life and

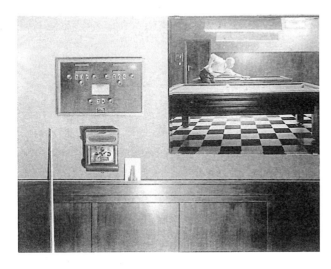

death: "Tis all a Chequer-board of Nights and Days / Where Destiny with Men for Pieces plays: / Hither and thither moves, and mates, and slays, / And one by one back in the Closet lays.'

Bound up with the theme of death is that of passing, past and lost time, which is suspended in the works of Jan Peter Tripp exactly as in Proust's novel before him, in that ephemeral moments and configurations are taken out of their sequence. A red glove, a burnt-out matchstick, a pearl onion on a chopping-board, such things then contain the whole of time: are salvaged, as it were, for ever by the painter's impassioned and patient work. The aura of remembrance that surrounds them lends them the character of mementoes in which melancholy crystallizes itself. An interior from La Cadière d'Azur shows a whitewashed wall and part of a darkened oleograph with the motif, just identifiable, of a boat passage across water. To the wide plaster frame, looking like passe-partout, of the oleograph a miniature painting on ivory is attached, a head and shoulders painting quite literally, because the face of the subject is scratched beyond recognition, and nothing else to be seen but the blue-uniformed torso of the strange hero. Also attached to the frame there is a little sprig of dried flowers — it reminded me at once of the good-fortune wreath woven by Karoline von Schlieben together with Heinrich von Kleist on the Brühl Terrace in Dresden on 16th May 1801, a photograph of which has been preserved — as well as a strip torn from a diary with the date 15th May, the painter's birthday.

Time lost, the pain of remembering and the figure of death have there been assembled in a memorial shrine as quotations from the painter's own life. Remembrance, after all, in essence is nothing other than a quotation. And the quotation incorporated in a text (or painting) by montage compels us — so Eco writes — to probe our knowledge of other texts and pictures and our knowledge of the world. This, in turn, takes time. By spending it, we enter into time recounted and into the time of culture. One final example of that is the picture *La Déclaration de guerre*, measuring 370 by 220 centimetres and showing an elegant pair of ladies' shoes that stand on a tiled floor. The pale blue/natural white ornament of the tiles, the grey lines of the joints, the lozenges cast by sunlight through a lead-framed window on to the picture's middle section, in which the black

shoes stand between two areas in shadow, all this together makes a geometric pattern of a complexity not to be rendered in words. This pattern, which enacts the degrees of difficulty of the various relations, connections, interweavings, and the mysterious pair of black shoes create a kind of picture puzzle, and one that a viewer ignorant of the pre-history can hardly solve. To what woman did those shoes belong? What became of her? Did the shoes pass into another person's possession? Or, ultimately, are they nothing more than the paradigm of that fetish which the painter is forced to make out of everything he produces? It's difficult to say more about this picture than that, in the teeth of its representational format and its seeming unambiguity, it encloses itself in the utmost privacy. The shoes don't give away their secret.

Two years later, it's true, the painter pushes his picture a little further at least into the public sphere. In a work very much smaller (100 by 145 centimetres), the larger painting reappears, not only as a quotation but as a mediating component of representation. Filling the upper two-thirds of the canvas, it now clearly hangs in its place; and in front of it, in front of *La Déclaration de guerre*, turning her back to the viewer, sideways on a white-upholstered mahogany chair, sits a flamingly red-haired woman. She is elegantly dressed, but still somehow tired by evening of the day's burdens. She has taken off one of her shoes — and they are the same that she contemplates on the large picture. Originally, so I was informed, she held this shoe taken off in her left hand, then it lay on the floor on the right, next to the chair, and finally it had wholly vanished. The woman with the one shoe, alone with herself and the enigmatic declaration of war, alone except for the faithful dog at her side, though this dog is not interested in the painted shoes but looks straight ahead out of the picture and into our eyes. An X-ray would show that earlier on he had once stood at the centre of the picture. Meanwhile

he has been out of doors and has brought in a sort
of wooden clog, from the fifteenth century or more
specifically from the wedding picture in the London
National Gallery that Jan van Eyck painted in 1434
for Giovanni Arnolfini and the Giovanna Cenami
affianced to him in a morganatic marriage 'of the left
hand', as a token of his witness. '*Johannes de Eyck
hic fuit*' we read on the frame of the round mirror in
which the scene, reduced to miniature format, can be
looked at once more, inverted. In the foreground, near
the left lower edge of the picture, lies that wooden
sandal, this curious piece of evidence, beside a little
dog that probably entered the picture as a symbol
of marital fidelity. The red-haired woman who in
Jan Peter Tripp's picture ponders the history of her
shoes and an inexplicable loss never guesses that the

disclosure of her secret lies behind her — in the shape of an anomalous object from a past world. The dog, bearer of the secret, who runs with ease over the abysses of time, because for him there is no difference between the fifteenth and the twentieth centuries, knows many things more accurately than we do. His left (domesticated) eye is attentively fixed on us; the right (wild) one has a little less light, strikes us as averted and alien. And yet we sense that it is the overshadowed eye that sees through us.

W. G. Sebald

Penetrating the Dark

So, when the optic nerve
tears, in the still space of the air
all turns as white as
the snow on the Alps

After Nature

The first thing that confronts us in the work of the writer W. G. Sebald is the face of St George on the left-hand panel of the Lindenhardt Altar of Matthias Grünewald: it is his own face, concealed by the painter in all his pictures. His face 'emerges again and again / in his work as that of a witness … / Always the same / gentleness, the same burden of grief, / the same irregularity of the eyes, veiled / and sliding sideways down into loneliness'. One does not need to have seen the last photographs of W. G. Sebald (one of whose Christian names was Georg) to recognize a sort of self-portrait in that description, and probably there is hardly a theme in his work as central to it as eyes are. It is with Grünewald's veiled gaze that the 'elemental poem' *After Nature*, Sebald's first published poetic work, begins. But the dimming of vision and the penetration of darkness are the key metaphors in all his books for his most intimate concern: the work of remembrance, the work of witness in the torrential flux of time.

In his last novel, *Austerlitz*, the narrator tells of a sudden loss of vision in the right eye. It seemed to him then 'as though at the edge of my field of vision I could see with undiminished clarity, as though I needed only to direct my attention to the periphery to put an end to what at first I judged to be a hysterical weakening of my sight'. This suggests that here the physical change responds to a psychic one, as though the eye had chosen to focus on the peripheral, on those things which the author was so intent on conserving, collecting and archivizing. Of the animals in the Nocturama which the narrator visits in the Antwerp Zoo right at the beginning of the novel, on the other hand, we are told 'that several of them had strikingly large eyes and that fixed, enquiring gaze found in certain painters and philosophers who seek to penetrate the darkness which surrounds us, purely by means of looking and thinking'. At this point, as so often in Sebald's books, we find four little photographic insets, details that show us four pairs of eyes – of a little owl and a larger owl, of Ludwig Wittgenstein and the painter Jan Peter Tripp, whose peering eyes look at us in this book too, from out of the dark, almost as though exposed by a lightning flash.

The painters Holbein and Grünewald, Sebald writes in the opening section of his long poem *After Nature*, 'in ... works of art ... / often made monuments in each other's / image where their paths had crossed'. The paths of W. G. Sebald and Jan Peter Tripp had crossed almost half a century ago and, in his last books especially, Sebald set a memorial to the painter of their lasting exchanges of glances. The project of a joint book arose several years ago; their declared aim was that text and image should not explain, let alone illustrate, each other but enter into a dialogue that would leave each his own space for reverberations. Until shortly before his death Sebald sent such texts to his friend in Alsace, though their final selection and collation was done by Jan Peter Tripp alone. The order and rhythm, however, obeyed the aesthetic demands of the material itself. Now this poem of gazes has become a memorial, a bequeathal.

W. G. Sebald died on 14th December 2001. And if this author never tired of tracing the destinations of his soulmates among writers, outsiders and emigrants in his sentences endlessly meandering through space and time, this legacy of his has the density of epitaphs. These are neither aphorisms nor poems, but rather flashes of thought and remembrance, moments of illumination on the verges of perception: metaphorical miniatures from the 'becalmed bay of the heart' in which Sebald cast anchor in his very first book, *After Nature*. Some of these texts are like photographs, snapshots that salvage a fleeting thing from the general flux. 'How curiously grey / was the light / when in March we / were on the river island

/ called Peacock Isle', impressions developed only later in the darkroom of memory, 'blue / grass / seen / through a thin / layer / of frozen / water'. They include personal addresses, requests for ascertainment, this or that throwaway, slightly distanced, defamiliarized mirror image: 'In the dining-car / of the Arlberg Express / sits a man / with a mourning lapel / & calmly, carefully / consumes his / Milanese cutlet.'

A ceremonial attentiveness, a literary work with that mourning lapel characterized a writer impelled by the realization that 'the world, as it were, depletes itself, because the stories that adhere to things are never heard by anyone, never recorded or retold', to quote *Austerlitz* once more. That 'inanimate' objects know more about us than we know about them Sebald remarked in his essay on the pictures of Jan Peter Tripp, whose 'deeply searching objectivity' he ascribed to that *'regard pré-humain'* which (according to Merleau-Ponty) reverses the direction of our looking. 'Looking,' Sebald writes in his book of essays *Logis in einem Landhaus*, 'the painter [Jan Peter Tripp] relinquishes our too facile knowingness; unrelatedly, things look across to us.'

The preparation of moments, time lost and time recovered, is the theme shared by the two artists, whose obsession with *The Reverse Side of Things* — the title of Tripp's earliest catalogue of works — is combined with the most precise representation of them that is possible; which means that the stupendous exactness in his pictures stands in an inverse ratio to the degree of their destructibility. Also, this love of the marginal clearly has a hidden counterpart in that region of the psyche that drove authors like Robert Walser or Kafka into minuteness and disappearance: both Tripp and Sebald have commemorated these two authors in their works. No wonder that Sebald found in Tripp's pictures the 'night-side vanishing point' beyond that threshold those are compelled to cross who have once engaged with the impassioned patience that is a painter's work. On his way there Sebald was arrested by the dead hyrax or cony which Tripp, 'in the thick of the chloroform vapour of putrefaction', preserved for ever in a *nature morte* during seven days of the year 1998. 'The black patch of fur around the eyes' of the dead animal, Sebald wrote in his essay, 'has the effect of a mourning crape or of the dark sleeping-glasses of an air passenger on a summer night's crossing of the North Pole.' Such summer night flights occur frequently in Sebald's books, and it cannot be ruled out that this hyrax merged in the animal – 'seven-times-sleeper' in German, 'dormouse' in English – that casts its deathly shadow in these miniatures too.

Much as the painter withdraws things from time and gives them the melancholy aura of mementoes, these last texts of Sebald's function as inscriptions, memorials and quotations. Inconspicuously, Sebald impregnated his great work of archivization with the tracks of his own biography and converted the date of his birth into an epitaph or 'scratched it on the cold limestone walls of the bunker', as at the end of *Austerlitz* the date of death of a victim of National Socialism: 'Max Stern, 18/5/1944.' That is the date of Sebald's birth. In 'the curious battle of Frankenhausen' mentioned in *After Nature*, 'in mid-May' an army of five thousand peasants lost their lives. 'When Grünewald got news of this / on the 18th of May / he ceased to leave his house. / Yet he could hear the gouging out / of eyes that long continued / between Lake Constance and / the Thuringian Forest. / For weeks at that time he wore / a dark bandage over his face.'

The motif of eyes in Sebald's work is bound up with the shadow of the war in the last year in which he was born: because his baptismal names Winfried Georg were 'too German' for him, he chose his third Christian name, Max. In the stories of *The Emigrants* it is the eyes of the Jewish painter Max Aurach, which the narrator came across by chance in a periodical and which had opened up for him that 'oubliette from which he will never escape'. Again and again the first-person narrator studies 'Aurach's dark eye, which in one of the photographs added to the text gazed into remoteness' and tries to explain to himself why he had once avoided asking the painter about his biography. And if the gradual dimming of the eyes of the half-Jewish Paul Bereyter, later a suicide, in the same volume is connected with an almost compulsively recurring memory of the Nazi era, the fading of his sight is also accompanied by a certain 'sense of comfort'. We hear something like it from the narrator of *Austerlitz*, who can't help associating the loss of sight with 'a vision of redemption' in which 'liberated from the endless need to write and read, I saw myself sit in a garden wicker chair, surrounded by a contourless world now recognizable only by its faded colours'.

In view of Sebald's reiterated complaints about 'the hard business of writing' one can't quite suppress the supposition that in these poetic miniatures the author wrote his way to the brink of silence. The longer he was away from his homeland, the more thoroughly Sebald transformed himself into that lonely wanderer who turns his back on us in the last photographs, while with hat and stick he makes towards a bend behind which, at the next moment, he will vanish. It is the same pedestrian who runs through all his books, a walker like Robert Walser, in whom Sebald, in an essay, recognized his beloved grandfather; it is that 'Max' whom Jan Peter Tripp shows us on the cover in half-profile. In a manner very similar Tripp had once depicted the portrait bust of a younger Robert Walser, with the same bushy moustache, with collar, cravat and a gaze directed to an imaginary distance. Only, this distance in either belongs to different regions; with Walser to the resounding emptiness of a boundless future opening out before him, with Sebald to a periphery beyond all sense of direction. It looks as though the painter had placed a silver veil over the iris.

Much as Sebald's segments as a whole convey the melody of a melancholic litany, Tripp's pairs of eyes always render the whole face, whether clear or threatened by a darkening, vulnerable or inviolable. The vividness that exceeds every kind of photographic precision, though, arises from Tripp's inclusion in the eye portraiture of the motions by which a person turns round, lowers the eyelids, shakes his/her head or speaks. The painter shows how people see, the poet how the perception shapes the world around them. So this dialogue between text and etching also becomes an exchange of looks between poets and painters, between the living and the dead. It follows the rhythm of a blink, the dramaturgy of light and shade, dream and waking, seeing and being seen, where it is not the contrast but the transition that matters, the path that each night we take over the threshold, till morning opens our eyelids. Rarely does a gaze focus on us as directly as those of the painter in the third picture or Justine's child's gaze that emerges entirely from wakefulness. Rather it seems at times as though the eyes, conversely, sucked in our seeing, as though they saw themselves in our light. The almond eyes of Ingres's Comtesse d'Haussonville, wholly at rest in their secrecy, look into a distance that knows nothing of a being-looked-at, the blind eyes of Borges look as though time had gathered inside them, far beyond those that see these eyes.

'Like a dog / Cézanne says / that's how a painter / must see, the eye / fixed & almost / averted.' Jan Peter Tripp has juxtaposed these lines with the shaded eyes of Rembrandt. The lines allude to a little text by Tripp about *Things*, but the dog runs into this book straight out of earlier pictures by Jan Peter Tripp. As a 'bearer of the secret' who, as Sebald writes in his essay on the painter, 'runs with ease over the abysses of time', a dog, he writes, knows 'many things more accurately than we do. His left (domesticated) eye is attentively fixed on us; the right (wild) one has a little less light, strikes us as averted and alien. And yet we sense that it is the overshadowed eye that sees through us.' Made for the penetration of the dark, though, the raptor's eye of that author stares out who may have plumbed the abyss more deeply than any other. To Beckett's eyes, which like bright knife-blades seem to cut through darkness, one of the most consoling verses in Sebald's work – a variation of Goethe's 'Wayfarer's Night Song' and a message to an unknown recipient – responds: 'He will cover / you with his / plumage / & / under his wing then / you will rest.'

Andrea Köhler